1-7-19 wavy pages

FENCING
FOR FUN!

by Suzanne Slade

Content Adviser: Laurence Schiller, Ph.D., Head Fencing Coach, Northwestern University;
Commissioner, Midwest Fencing Conference; Vice President, U.S. Fencing Coaches' Association Midwest;
Vice Chair, United States Fencing Association, Illinois Division
Reading Adviser: Frances J. Bonacci, Ed.D., Reading Specialist, Cambridge, Massachusetts

Compass Point Books ✦ Minneapolis, Minnesota

Compass Point Books
151 Good Counsel Drive
P.O. Box 669
Mankato, MN 56002-0669

This book was manufactured with paper containing at least 10 percent post-consumer waste.

Photographs ©: Laurent Fievet/Getty Images Inc., cover, 6; Pedro Jorge Henriques Monteiro/Shutterstock, back cover, 42 (left); The Granger Collection, New York, 4; William Attard McCarthy/Shutterstock, 5; 2008 Jupiterimages Corporation, 8 (left); Nicholas Rjabow/Shutterstock, 8–9, 45 (left); Torsten Blackwood/AFP/Getty Images, 9; jaymast/Shutterstock, 10 (all); Creatas/SuperStock, 11 (top); Corbis/SuperStock, 11 (bottom); PhotoCreate/Shutterstock, 12–13; MCales/Shutterstock, 13 (right); SuperStock, 14; Image Source/Getty Images, 15; Image Source/SuperStock, 16; Photodisc, 17, 28–29; ThinkStock/SuperStock, 18; Alaistar Grant/AP Images, 19; Digital Vision, 20–21; Stockbyte/SuperStock, 22–23 (all), 47; Photodisc/SuperStock, 24; Vincenzo Pinto/AFP/Getty Images, 25; Zefa/SuperStock, 26–27; Streeter Lecka/Getty Images for DAGOC, 27 (right); Martin Rose/Getty Images for DAGOC, 30 (bottom); Wm. Baker/GhostWorx Images/Alamy, 30–31; Thomas Coex/AFP/Getty Images, 32; Serge Timacheff/Corbis, 33; Maxim Marmur/AFP/Getty Images, 34 (bottom); Hassan Ammar/AFP/Getty Images, 34–35; Giuseppe Cacace/AFP/Getty Images, 36; Margot Petrowski/Shutterstock, 37; Aubrey Washington/Allsport/Getty Images, 38; John Amis/AP Images, 39; Central Press/Hulton Archive/Getty Images, 40–41 (bottom); Donald Miralle/Getty Images, 40–41 (top); IOC/Allsport/Getty Images, 41; IOC/Olympic Museum/Allsport/Getty Images, 42 (right); Popperfoto/Getty Images, 43 (left); Brian Bahr/Allsport/Getty Images, 43 (bottom right); Joel Saget/AFP/Getty Images, 43 (top right); Getty Images, 44; Shariffc/Dreamstime, 45 (right).

Editor: Brenda Haugen
Page Production: The Design Lab
Photo Researcher: Robert McConnell
Art Director: LuAnn Ascheman-Adams
Creative Director: Keith Griffin
Editorial Director: Nick Healy
Managing Editor: Catherine Neitge

Acknowledgment: Special thanks to Gordon Gandy, coach of the Crimson Blades Fencing Academy, for sharing his fencing expertise and enthusiasm for this book.

Library of Congress Cataloging-in-Publication Data
Slade, Suzanne.
  Fencing for fun! / by Suzanne Slade.
     p. cm. — (For fun)
  Includes index.
  ISBN 978-0-7565-3866-8 (library binding)
  1. Fencing—Juvenile literature. I. Title. II. Series.
  GV1147.S59 2009
  796.86—dc22   2008005737

Visit Compass Point Books on the Internet at www.compasspointbooks.com
or e-mail your request to custserv@compasspointbooks.com

Table of Contents

Note: In this book, there are two kinds of vocabulary words. Fencing Words to Know are words specific to fencing. They are defined on page 46. Other Words to Know are helpful words that are not related only to fencing. They are defined on page 47.

The Art of Sword Fighting

Have you ever pretended to be a pirate who duels enemies with a sword? Do you dream of being a knight who uses a sword to slay dragons? Books and movies are full of sword-fighting heroes such as these. In fencing, you can learn to handle a swordlike weapon with skill.

People have been sword fighting, or fencing, for thousands of years. The first known organized fencing method began in Germany in the 14th century. In the city of Frankfurt, German fencers called the Marxbruder started a university for those interested in the sport. These early swordsmen used large, heavy weapons for fighting.

A shorter, lighter weapon was developed in the 18th century. It allowed fencers to move much faster. With this new weapon, the quicker, more modern type of fencing was born.

Fencing Competitions

A fencing match between two people is called a bout. A fencer scores a point, called a touch, by using his or her weapon to touch his or her opponent's target area.

Bouts are timed and are usually fought to either five or 15 touches. If time runs out before either fencer reaches the required number of touches, the person with the most touches wins. If the bout is tied when time runs out, the fencers compete in an overtime period. In overtime, the first fencer to score a touch wins.

Fencing also can be a team sport. Fencers from each team compete in several bouts. The fencers' results are added to their teams' total scores.

Fencing Inside the Lines

Fencing is done inside a rectangular area called a strip. A fencing strip is 14 meters (46 feet) long and 2 meters (6.5 feet) wide. A centerline across the middle divides the strip into two sides.

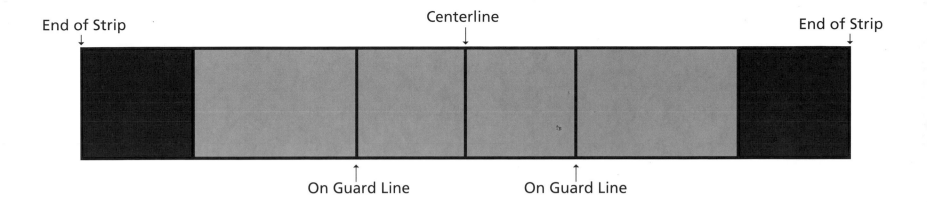

End of Strip　　　　　　　Centerline　　　　　　　End of Strip

On Guard Line　　　　On Guard Line

There are two on guard lines. Each on guard line is 2 meters (6.5 feet) from the centerline on each side of a strip. Fencers stand behind their on guard lines before a fencing bout begins. During a bout, fencers must stay in the strip.

The line at each end of the strip is called the end line. A colored 2-meter zone warns the fencer that he or she is nearing the end line. If both of a fencer's feet go behind the end line during a bout, his or her opponent scores a touch.

Types of Strips

A fencing strip is usually made of metal. Some schools and gyms have permanent strips painted on their floors. If they don't have metal or painted strips, tape may be used to create strips for fencing.

Foil, Épée, Saber

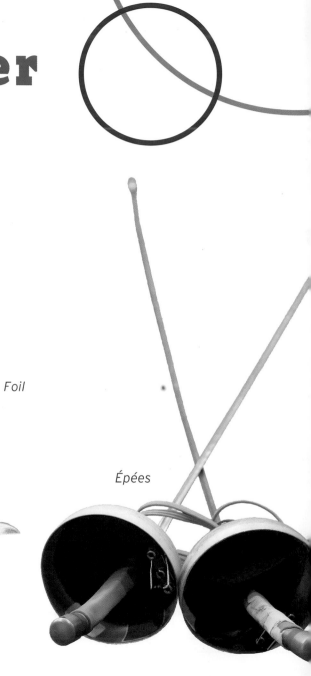

There are three fencing weapons—the foil, the épée, and the saber. Each type of weapon is different, but all have bendable blades with blunt tips.

The foil is the lightest of the three types of fencing weapons. The target area for the foil is the torso. A foil fencer uses the tip of the blade to touch a rival's target area and score a point.

An épée (pronounced *e-PAY*) is the heaviest fencing weapon. The target area when fencing with an épée is the entire body. Épée fencers use their blade tips to make touches.

Foil

Épées

8

Saber fencer

In saber bouts, the target area is from the waist up and includes the head and arms. Hands are not part of the target area. To score a touch, saber fencers can slash an opponent's target area with the side of the blade as well as touch the target area with the blade tip.

Some teachers suggest that beginners learn with foils first, but this is not a rule. A new fencer can start with any weapon.

Holding Your Weapon

In order to make controlled blade movements, you should hold your weapon by pinching the top of the handle with your thumb and index finger. Your other three fingers simply curl around the end of the handle.

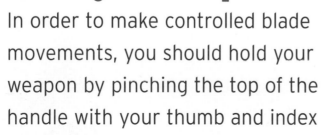

Gearing Up

Fencers must wear the proper gear to protect their bodies. Most fencing teachers provide basic equipment for beginners. If you continue to fence—or want to compete—you will have to buy your own gear. You only need a few items to get started.

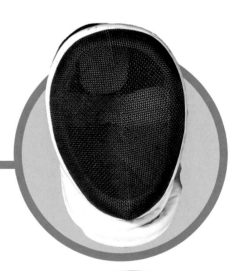

Mask: A fencing mask is made of strong metal mesh that a fencer can see through. The mask covers the front, sides, and top of a fencer's head. The inside of the mask is padded to make it more comfortable. The lower part of the mask includes a tough fabric bib to protect the fencer's neck.

Glove: A fencing glove is made of stretchy fabric. These gloves provide padding on the back of fencers' hands and protect them from bruises.

Jacket: The thick, heavy fabric of a fencing jacket protects a fencer's chest, arms, and back from an opponent's hits. With its high neckline, a fencing jacket provides some protection for the neck area. An adjustable strap on the bottom of a fencing jacket creates a snug fit. Female fencers also must wear plastic chest protectors under their jackets.

Weapon: The blade of a fencing weapon is made of specially treated metals so it is strong, yet bendable. A lightweight metal guard above the handle protects the fencer's hand.

Other Gear

Most fencers start with the basic equipment and add items as they become more serious about the sport. Other gear you may want in the future might include white fencing pants called knickers, long white socks, and a pair of fencing shoes, which are lighter than most other shoes.

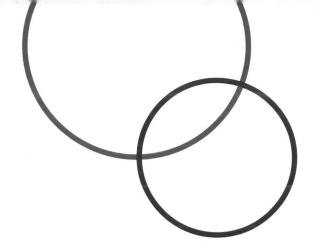

Using Mind and Body

Fencing is a mental and physical game. Fencers sometimes call the sport a game of physical chess. In fencing, competitors must anticipate their opponents' moves as they carefully plan their own moves—just like in a game of chess. A fencer needs to make quick decisions to stop his or her opponent from scoring or to find just the right place to attack.

Your body also must be well-trained to succeed in fencing. Strength and speed allow a fencer to make a quick touch and to avoid being hit. A fencer who is in good shape will be able to compete in several bouts without tiring.

Benefits of the Sport

Fencing helps people improve their balance, coordination, and reflexes. Fencing also teaches people many things that can be helpful in other areas of life. Fencers learn self-control and how to be good sports. They discover how to solve problems and make quick decisions, too.

Making the Touch

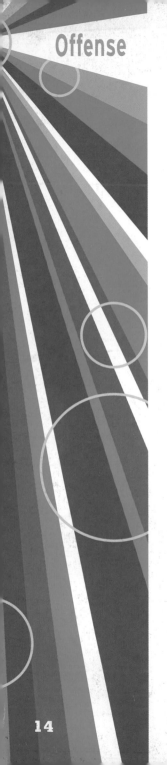

A fencer who has a plan of attack is more likely to get touches and win a bout than a fencer who tries random attacks. Pay attention to the moves your opponent often uses. Knowing these favorite moves can help you identify the blade motion your opponent is starting to make. If you can figure out your rival's next move, you will know what part of his or her target area will be unprotected. Then you can attack that area.

Always be aware of how far you are from your opponent. To be a winning fencer, you must be close enough to your opponent when you begin your attack to make a touch.

Safety First

Weapons must be handled with great care. When you carry your weapon, keep the point down by your side. Don't play with your weapon. It should only be used when you and those around you are wearing the proper protection.

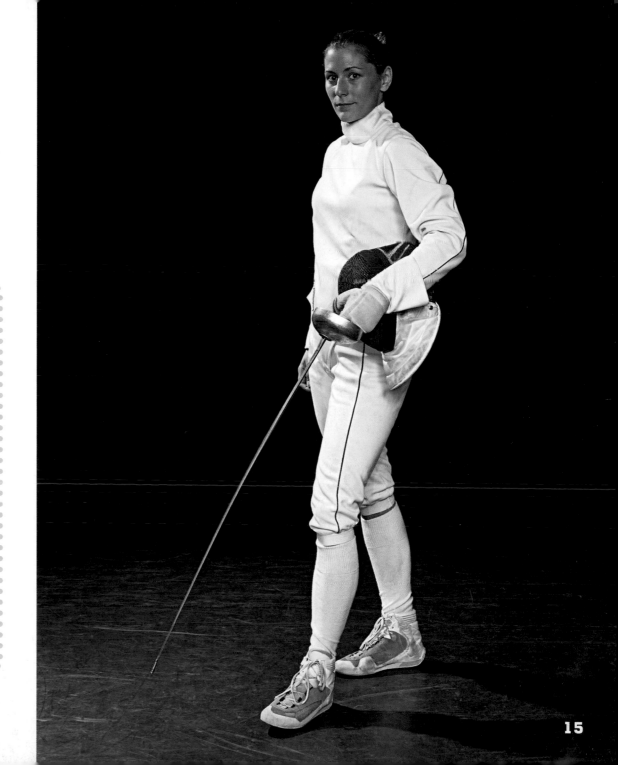

Avoiding a Hit

A strong offense helps a fencer earn touches, but a good defense is also important to win a bout. A solid defense keeps your opponent from scoring touches. To avoid giving touches to your rival, you need to stay alert and protect your target area.

Your first line of defense is to block your opponent's weapon with your blade. Notice your rival's movements. A quick reaction using fast arm movement will help you stop an incoming weapon.

Another way to avoid giving points to your opponent is to stay out of his or her reach. Fast footwork is important. If you can move back quickly, you may be able to avoid an opponent's touch. But be careful not to move past the end line or your opponent will be awarded a point.

Heads Up!

Sometimes a beginning fencer is tempted to bend forward, hiding his or her face, when an opponent attacks near his or her head. This is unsafe because a fencing mask does not cover the back of the head. Fencers need to keep their heads up during bouts.

Showing Respect

One of the oldest traditions in fencing is the salute. A fencer salutes his or her opponent as a sign of respect. In fencing competitions all over the world, fencers must salute before a bout begins. Fencers also salute their opponents before shaking hands at the ends of bouts.

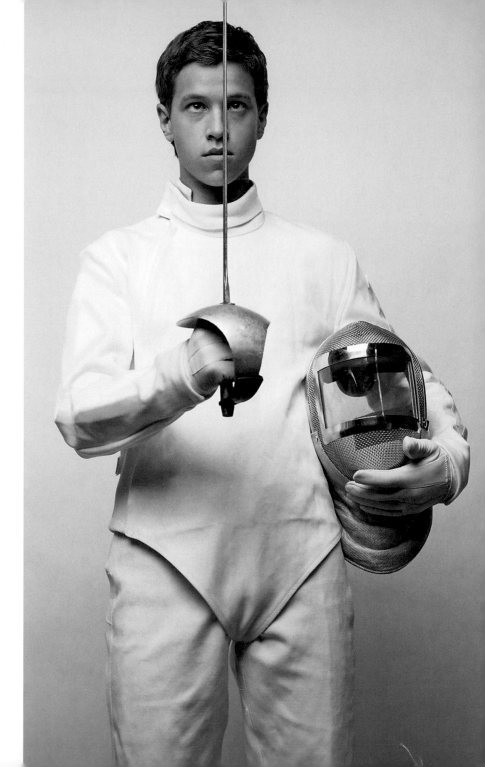

To give a proper salute, you must stand tall as you face your opponent. Hold your weapon a few inches from the ground. Hold your mask in your other hand. Now raise your weapon hand to your chin so your blade points straight up. Next, move the blade quickly toward your opponent and then back toward the ground where it was before.

Remember the Referee!

Fencers often salute the referee before a bout. The referee controls the action on the strip. He or she decides which fencer wins the touch for each action during a bout. The referee also calls penalties when fencers break the rules.

Ready to Fence

One of the first things a new fencer learns is how to stand in the on guard position. In this position, a fencer is alert and ready to move.

It may be helpful to face a mirror as you follow the steps to learn the on guard position. (These directions are for a right-handed fencer. Left-handed fencers should use the opposite feet and hands.)

1. Turn your body slightly sideways so your right shoulder is forward. Put your hands on your hips.

2. Move your heels together, and position your feet so they are at a 90-degree angle to each other. This is called the ready position.

3. Step forward with your right foot about 1 ½ foot lengths, and bend your knees.

4. Check your balance by lifting the toes of your front foot and the heel of your back foot. If you can do this, you are not leaning too far forward or too far back.

5. Move your left arm back, bending it so your hand is over your shoulder. Now you're in the on guard position and ready to fence.

Stay in Balance
A fencer in the on guard position must stay balanced at all times. You can achieve this goal by evenly putting your body weight on both feet and keeping your arms in the proper positions.

Fancy Footwork

When a fencer steps toward an opponent, this is called an advance. Advancing lets fencers move close enough to their opponents that they can reach them with their weapons.

To advance, start in your on guard position with your feet at a 90-degree angle to each other. Then lift your front foot, toes first, and move it forward a few inches. Taking small steps helps you keep your balance. Keep both knees bent as you move your back foot forward the same distance. Repeat these steps quickly to advance. As you advance, do not lift either foot more than 1 inch (2.5 centimeters) from the floor.

Practice Makes Perfect!

This basic footwork may seem simple at first, but a skilled fencer practices these steps often. Learning the correct way to advance and retreat will help you move quickly and keep the correct distance between you and your opponent during a bout.

When a fencer steps backward, away from an opponent, this is called a retreat. A quick retreat helps a fencer avoid being hit. Fencers also retreat to encourage their opponents to move forward.

To retreat, move your rear foot back a few inches. Then quickly move your front foot back the same distance. While retreating, keep your knees bent. Your feet should stay close to the ground and about a shoulder's width apart.

Fast Forward

A lunge is a big, quick step forward. This move allows a fencer to make a powerful attack and score a touch.

To begin a lunge, stand in the on guard position. Then step forward by lifting your front foot, toes first. As you step with your front foot, keep your back foot in place, and push forward with your back leg muscles. Extend your back leg fully, and land on the heel of your front foot. The knee of your front leg should line up straight above your shoelaces.

During a lunge, your weapon hand should be moving forward, staying slightly ahead of your front foot. When a lunge is completed, your weapon should be extended in front of your body. Your other hand should be back over your rear leg.

You will need to practice the lunge many times to get the proper timing down. Once you have mastered this forceful step, you can combine it with weapon moves to create an effective attack.

Stretch Before You Fence

Be sure to stretch out before practicing your fencing moves. An instructor can show you the proper way to stretch your arm, back, and leg muscles. Leg stretches are especially important before lunging.

Hitting the Target

To win a fencing bout, you must score touches by hitting your opponent's target area. Fencers have many different attacks to choose from to achieve that goal. The following are some of the simplest and most common fencing attacks.

Straight attack: To do a straight attack, extend your weapon arm straight out in front of you as you lunge forward toward your opponent.

Beat attack: To carry out a beat attack, quickly hit the middle of your opponent's blade with your blade to knock it out of the way before performing a straight attack.

Disengage: A disengage is used when your opponent tries to beat, or hit, your blade. If you see a beat coming, quickly drop and then lift your blade tip so your rival will miss your blade. Then thrust your blade forward, and hit your target.

Think Fast!

A successful attack begins with fast thinking. A fencer must quickly examine his opponent's body position and movements to choose an attack that will hit the target.

Blocking the Blade

What should you do if a rival's blade is heading straight toward your target area? You can parry. This is blocking your opponent's blade with your blade.

There are eight parry moves. Each parry protects a certain part of your body. For example, a Parry 1 protects the lower, inside part of your target. To do a Parry 1, hold your weapon in front of the lower right inside part of your body with the blade pointing down.

A fencing teacher can show you all the parry moves for the type of fencing you choose. Fencers practice parries so often that they become almost automatic during a bout.

Different Weapons, Different Moves

Not all parries are used for every weapon. Foil and épée fencers have more parries than saber fencers do.

And some of the parries vary a bit, depending on which weapon you are using.

Get Hooked Up

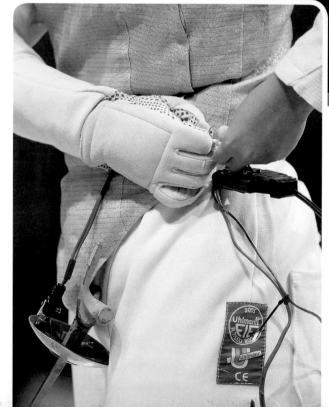

Weapons move quickly during a fencing bout. Often both fencers' blades touch their rivals' targets at about the same time. It can be hard for a referee to see which fencer won the touch. Electric fencing equipment is used to help decide these close calls.

In electric fencing, foil and saber fencers wear lames, which are thin outer jackets that cover their target areas. Lames are made from fabric that conducts electricity. When a fencer touches an opponent's lame with his or her blade, an electronic signal is sent to the scoring box. A colored light goes on to signal a touch. A white light signals when a hit is made outside of the target area. In épée,

the whole body is the target, so épée fencers do not need to wear lames. A signal is sent to the scoring box from the épée any time a touch is made.

But the referee—not the lights—makes the final decision on who scores a point. The referee follows the rule of right-of-way. Under this rule, the fencer who started to attack first earns the touch if he or she hits an opponent's target area. The fencer who is being attacked must defend himself or herself with a parry or cause his or her rival to miss before taking over right-of-way and scoring a touch. A fencer who takes too long to advance while attacking his or her opponent also gives up the right-of-way to the opponent.

The Beginning of Electric Fencing

In 1936, an engineering student at Columbia University named Alfred Skrobisch invented the electronic scoring box. Épée was the first electric weapon and was used at the 1936 Berlin Olympic Games. Foil became electric in the 1950s, but saber did not become electric until the 1990s.

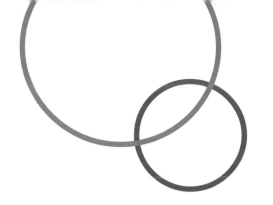

Facing Your Opponent

Before every bout, fencers stand behind their on guard lines and salute each other. Then they put on their masks and stand in the on guard position. Next the referee calls out, "On guard, ready, fence!"

At the "fence" command, the competitors begin fencing until the referee calls "Halt!"

This call is often made when a fencer gets a touch. If a hit is scored, the referee will explain the action, award the touch, and give the bout score. If you notice something that could be dangerous during a bout—such as an untied shoelace or a broken blade—you should get the referee's attention right away so he or she will stop the match.

A referee may also call a halt if there is an off-target hit, if a fencer leaves the strip, or if a fencer commits an offense. An offense is an action that affects the safety of the fencers or when a fencer shows poor sportsmanship. A referee may give a fencer a card and a penalty for an offense.

Cards and Penalties

During a bout, a fencer may receive a warning and a yellow card for an offense such as going outside the strip. After a second offense, the fencer may be given a red card and lose a point. For serious offenses that affect safety—such as hitting too hard—a fencer may immediately receive a red or black card. A black card means the fencer must leave the strip and the tournament.

Mind Your Manners

Fencers should show good fencing manners at all times. An important part of fencing etiquette is competing fairly. Courteous fencers make sure all of their electric cords are connected and working properly. Proper fencing conduct also includes controlling your emotions. A fencer should not show anger or disappointment on the strip.

Everybody Wins

A fencer who wants to learn and have fun during a bout always comes out a winner. As you compete, you will improve your skills and get some great exercise. So enjoy the sport of fencing—win or lose!

Fencing is a sport of tradition and honor. Good fencing manners require fencers to remove their masks when they salute at the beginning of bouts and at the end when they shake hands. You should always congratulate your rival at the end of a bout to show respect for a well-fought match.

Join in the Fun!

If you like fencing, you may want to join a fencing club. Club members learn fencing skills and strategies from a coach. You also can make new friends and practice with fencers at different skill levels.

Club members often travel together to tournaments. They help each other at fencing events by scouting the strengths and weaknesses of rivals and sharing that information with their teammates. They also may help with gear. If a fencer has equipment problems, another team member may be able to fix it or loan a piece of gear. Club members also show their support by cheering for one another during bouts.

It's fun to have friends who enjoy the same activity you do. If you're looking for some fencing friends, ask an adult to help you search the Internet for a club near you.

Find a Club

If you want to join a fencing club, you may be able to find one on the Web. Using your favorite search engine, type in the words fencing clubs. Many clubs are listed online.

The Greats

Felicia Zimmerman (right) is a top women's fencer in both foil and épée. She entered her first fencing tournament when she was 8 years old. She went on to win seven gold medals and one silver medal at the Junior Olympics. When she was 21, Zimmerman was the first American woman to win a gold medal at a junior World Cup. She also represented the United States at the 1996 and 2000 Olympics.

Peter Westbrook competed in fencing tournaments around the world for nearly 30 years. During his career, this fierce saber fencer won 13 national championships. In 1989, Westbrook was a finalist at the world championships. He was also a member of six U.S. Olympic fencing teams. He won a bronze medal at the 1984 Olympics.

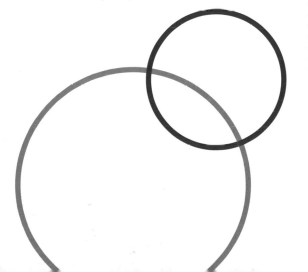

A Winner off the Strip

In 1991, Peter Westbrook (below, left) started a program to help inner-city children in New York. At the Peter Westbrook Foundation, children receive fencing training along with homework help. Professional athletes and other famous people often visit the foundation to encourage students to work hard. Because of Westbrook's help, thousands of children have become successful students as well as good fencers.

Bouting With the Best

Fencing was part of the first Olympic Games in ancient Greece. When the modern Olympics began in 1896 in Athens, fencing was included in the Games. That year, fencers from France, Greece, and Denmark competed for medals in foil and saber. At the 1900 Olympics in Paris, an épée event was added. The United States earned its first fencing medals at the 1904 games.

Female fencers were not included in the Olympics for many years. In 1924, women's foil became an official Olympic event. Ellen Osiier from Denmark won the gold medal that year. Women's épée was added in 1996. Women's saber was included in 2004. Today men and women fencers around the world train hard with the hope of winning Olympic medals in the sport.

Triple Threat

Italian fencer Nedo Nadi (right) won gold medals in foil, épée, and saber at the 1920 Olympic Games. Interestingly, Nadi's father had forbidden him to learn épée because he said it was an "undisciplined" weapon. Nadi used to sneak out of the house to practice épée anyway.

What Happened When?

| 1300 | 1800 | 1850 | 1900 | 1910 |

1300s A fencing university is set up in Frankfurt, Germany.

1891 The Amateur Fencers League of America is formed.

1904 U.S. fencers earn their first Olympic fencing medals in St. Louis, Missouri.

1820s The fencing mask is accepted and worn by most fencers.

1896 Men's foil fencing is included in the first modern Olympic Games in Athens, Greece.

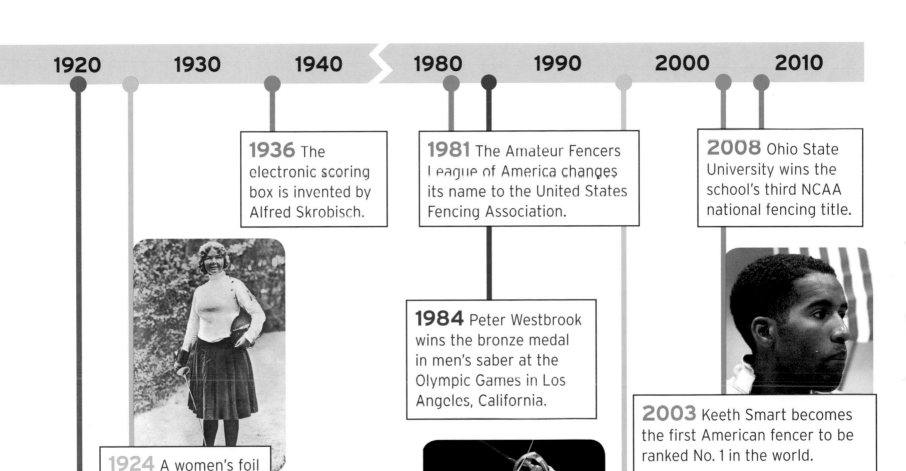

1920   **1930**   **1940**   **1980**   **1990**   **2000**   **2010**

1936 The electronic scoring box is invented by Alfred Skrobisch.

1981 The Amateur Fencers League of America changes its name to the United States Fencing Association.

2008 Ohio State University wins the school's third NCAA national fencing title.

1984 Peter Westbrook wins the bronze medal in men's saber at the Olympic Games in Los Angeles, California.

2003 Keeth Smart becomes the first American fencer to be ranked No. 1 in the world.

1924 A women's foil event is added to the Olympic Games.

1920 Nedo Nadi wins Olympic gold medals in the foil, épée, and saber events.

1996 A women's épée event is added to the Olympic Games; women's saber competition is added in 2004.

Fun Fencing Facts

A 4,000-year-old carving of two fencers dueling with blunt swords was found in a temple in Egypt. There were also spectators, officials, and a scorekeeper pictured at the ancient match.

The long, narrow shape of the fencing strip comes from the tight places where early sword fighters often dueled, such as castle hallways.

Several modern movies feature action-packed fencing duels. Box-office hits such as *Hook*, *The Mask of Zorro*, and *Pirates of the Caribbean* have thrilled audiences with their exciting fencing scenes.

Did you ever wonder why fencers wear white? This color was originally chosen for function rather than fashion. Before electronic scoring was invented, fencers put cotton pieces soaked in ink on their weapon tips. Black ink spots on white uniforms made it easy to see touches.

More than half of the fencers in the United States Fencing Association are 15 years old or younger.

Fencing bouts were not given time limits until a master's championship bout in the 1930s lasted seven hours. Today a five-touch bout can last a maximum of three minutes. A 15-touch bout may continue up to nine minutes.

Fencing Words to Know

advance: taking a step toward one's opponent

attack: movement or series of movements a fencer uses to try to score a touch

beat: sharp tap on an opponent's blade that is used before an attack or to get a reaction

bout: one match, or game

end line: line found at each end of a fencing strip

épée: heaviest type of weapon used in fencing

foil: lightest type of weapon used in fencing

lame: jacket worn during an electric fencing bout

lunge: moving forward to attack an opponent quickly by pushing off from the back leg

on guard: position a fencer takes before a bout begins

on guard line: line 2 meters (6.5 feet) back from the centerline on each side of a fencing strip that fencers stand behind before a bout begins

parry: defensive action where a fencer blocks an opponent's blade with his or her own blade

saber: medium-weight weapon used in fencing

slash: blade movement used in saber fencing where a fencer strikes another with the side of the blade

strip: rectangular-shaped fencing area that is 14 meters (46 feet) long and 2 meters (6.5 feet) wide

target area: location on an opponent's body that must be hit to score a touch

touch: point scored in fencing

Other Words to Know

anticipate: expect ahead of time

blunt: not sharp

courteous: polite

random: no set pattern or order

scouting: watching competitors to discover their strengths and weaknesses

torso: trunk of the body from the neck to the waist but not including the arms

Where to Learn More

MORE BOOKS TO READ

Greenberg, Doreen. *Sword of a Champion: The Story of Sharon Monplaisir.* Terre Haute, Ind.: Wish Publishing, 2000.

Page, Jason. *Combat: Fencing, Judo, Wrestling, Boxing, Taekwondo, and Lots, Lots More.* Minneapolis: LernerSports, 2000.

ON THE ROAD

The Museum of American Fencing
1413 Fairfield Ave.
Shreveport, LA 71101
318/227-7575

The Fencers Club
229 W. 28th St.
New York, NY 10001
212/807-6947

ON THE WEB

For more information on this topic, use FactHound.

1. Go to *www.facthound.com*
2. Type in this book ID: 0756538661
3. Click on the *Fetch It* button.

FactHound will find the best Web sites for you.

INDEX

ABOUT THE AUTHOR

Suzanne Buckingham Slade is the author of many nonfiction and fiction books for children. She enjoys bike riding, sailing, and in-line skating. She also loves to watch her son, Patrick, duel in saber with great speed and skill.